The Story of
CREATION

To the children who still wonder, who still ask questions,
and who still want to know.

May your curiosity lead you to truth, your heart remain open to wisdom,
and your journey be filled with light.

This story is for you.

Copyright © 2025 by Fifth Ribb Publishing, LLC
All Rights Reserved. Printed in the United States of America
This book or any portion thereof may not be reproduced or used in any manner whatsoever without the express written permission of the publisher except for the use of brief quotations in critical articles and book reviews.
Fifth Ribb Publishing, LLC. 6951 Olive Blvd, University City, MO 63130
www.fifthribbpublishing.com

ISBN: 9781736789858

First Edition

The Story of CREATION

Written by Pamela Blair
Illustrated by Sameer Kassar

Fifth Ribb Publishing, LLC

In the Beginning

A long, long time ago, before the whisper of the wind or the sparkle of the stars, there was nothing. No earth beneath bare feet, no skies to stretch above, no rustling trees, no scurrying animals. Just a deep, velvety quiet. Only God and His angels filled the endless space.

One day, with a bright, knowing smile, God turned to His angels and said, "Shall we create something wonderful? A world bursting with light and life?" The angels clapped their hands in delight, their eyes shining with excitement. And so, the grand masterpiece began.

The First Day: Creating Day and Night

God smiled big and said, "Let there be light!" And—BOOM!—light filled the darkness. Everything glowed with warmth and light. The angels giggled and clapped. "When it's dark, we'll call it night," God said, "and when

the light comes, we'll call it day!" The angels danced, their wings sparkling in the bright new light.

God was pleased with what He had created, and He called that day good.

The Second Day: Creating Heaven and Earth

The next morning, God had something else to show. With a swoosh of His hand, He made the wind swirl around, spinning and twirling until the clouds popped up in the

sky, puffing and floating. "The top of these clouds will be heaven, and the bottom of the clouds will be Earth," God said with a grin. The angels couldn't believe it!

God was pleased with what He had created, and He called that day good.

The Third Day: Creating Land and Plants

On the third day, God gathered the waters into oceans, rivers, and seas. Then—whoosh!—He raised the land, forming mountains and grassy hills. At His word, trees and flowers sprang up—red roses, blue lilies, and golden sunflowers swayed in the breeze. Fruit trees heavy with

sweet, colorful mangoes, apples, and papayas filled the land. The angels clapped and sang as the world bloomed with life.

God was pleased with what He had created, and He called that day good.

The Fourth Day: Creating The Sun, Moon and Stars

The very next day, the angels came running, their wings fluttering in excitement. What would God create next? God said, "Let's add some light to the sky!" And with a big, happy wave, the sun appeared, shining brightly in the day sky, warming the Earth. Then, with another

wave, the moon appeared, glowing softly in the night sky. Twinkling stars popped up, filling the dark sky with magic and wonder. The angels danced in the soft moonlight and basked in the warmth of the sun, filled with joy.

God was pleased with What he had created and he called that day good.

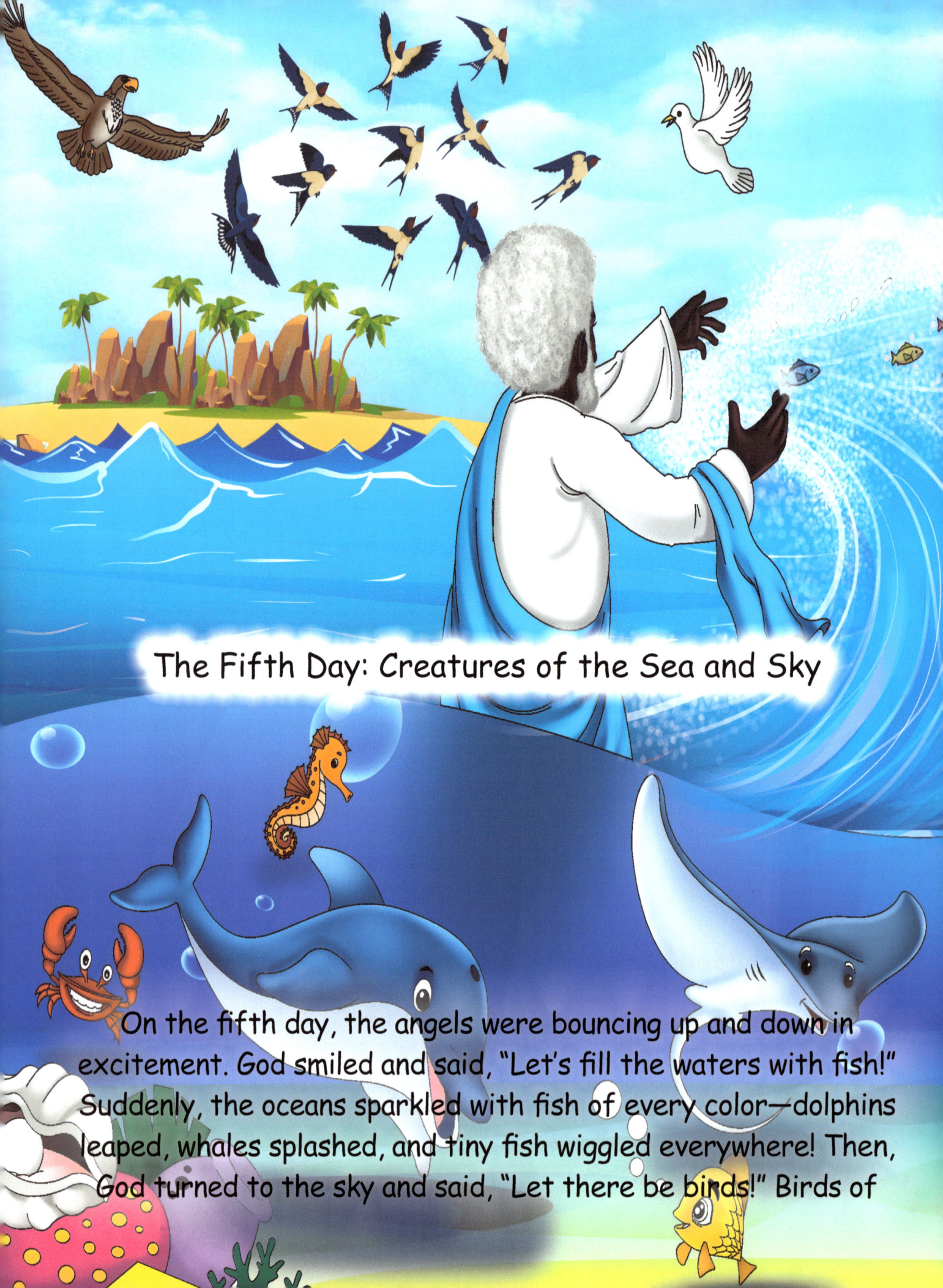

The Fifth Day: Creatures of the Sea and Sky

On the fifth day, the angels were bouncing up and down in excitement. God smiled and said, "Let's fill the waters with fish!" Suddenly, the oceans sparkled with fish of every color—dolphins leaped, whales splashed, and tiny fish wiggled everywhere! Then, God turned to the sky and said, "Let there be birds!" Birds of

every shape and color flapped their wings, and butterflies danced in the air. The angels laughed and cheered as they watched the sea creatures and flying friends spread across the world.

God was pleased with What he had created and he called that day good.

Giraffes stretched their long necks, and rabbits hopped across the grass. The angels were amazed at all the creatures!

Then, God said, "Let's make people who will be just like us." And so, from the earth, God created a man named Adam. But Adam was alone, so God made Eve from Adam's rib. Together, they explored their beautiful new home.

God was pleased with What he had created and he called that day good.

The Seventh Day: The Sabbath Day

After all the work of creating, God said, "It's time to rest." On the seventh day, everyone—God, the angels, and Adam and Eve—took a big, peaceful break. The world was full of beauty, and everyone rested in the quiet and

calm of the day. "This day is holy," said God. And from then on, every seventh day would be a day of rest, a time to enjoy the world and everything in it.

That day was good, and God called it The Sabbath Day.

God looked at everything He had made—the heavens, the earth, the seas, the animals, and the very first people—and was very pleased. "It is very good," He said, and the world was complete. And that's how the world

was made—so full of light, color, and life. The world was very good, and it was just the beginning of the most wonderful adventure yet!

Now It's Your Turn!

God made an amazing world, full of wonders, colors, and life. But guess what? There's still room for YOU to add something special to God's great creation!

What can you create? Maybe it's a beautiful drawing, a new game for your friends, a song, or even a kind action to help someone. Think of one thing you can do to make the world a better place and share the love and joy that God has given us.

What will YOU create today? Let your imagination soar and see how you can help make the world as wonderful as God intended it to be!

Vocabulary Words & Meanings

1. **Adventure** – An exciting and fun journey or experience. In the story, God and the angels went on an adventure to create the world.

2. **Twinkle** – A small, bright shine or sparkle. God's eyes twinkled when He came up with the idea to create the world.

3. **Glow** – A soft, warm light. The light that God made in the beginning filled the darkness and made everything glow.

4. **Swoosh** – A soft sound made when something moves quickly through the air. God made the wind swoosh and swirl to create the clouds.

5. **Whoosh** – A soft rushing sound, like wind or water. God made the land rise with a "whoosh!" from the water.

6. **Sparkling** – Shining brightly with small flashes of light. The angels' wings were sparkling in the new light.

7. **Trumpeted** – A loud, joyful sound made by some animals, like elephants. The elephants trumpeted happily in the new world.

8. **Holy** – Special and set apart for God. The seventh day was a holy day of rest, a time to enjoy the world.

9. **Rest** – To take a break and relax. After creating the world, God and everyone rested on the seventh day.

10. **Sabbath Day** – A special day of rest and worship. God made the seventh day holy and set it apart as a day of rest.

The Moral of the Story:

God created everything with love, care, and purpose. Each part of the world—light and dark, land and sea, animals and people—was made in perfect order. Nothing was rushed or random; everything had a reason.

This teaches us that God's creation has a purpose, and so do we! Just as the world works together in harmony, we are all part of His amazing plan. By living with order and purpose, we can honor our God's creation and make his world a better place.

Pamela Blair is an acclaimed author renowned for her compelling books inspired by Bible stories. Her writing journey began while homeschooling her children, driven by the desire to impart the knowledge of their biblical heritage. Faced with the absence of illustrated Bible stories featuring children who looked like her own, Pamela took it upon herself to create them.

Prior to delving into the world of Biblical narratives, Pamela earned an undergraduate degree in Business Management from Fairleigh Dickinson University. In addition to her writing endeavors, she is the proud owner of Eyeseeme Bookstore, a distinguished retail establishment that focuses on both fiction and nonfiction narratives celebrating the rich diversity of Black people worldwide.

With a steadfast commitment to family, Pamela has been happily married to Jeffrey Blair for 38 years. Together, they share the joys of parenthood with their four adult children: Jeffrey Jr, Naomi, Sarah, and Ezra. Pamela takes immense pride in her children, attributing their successes to an unwavering faith in God—The God of Abraham, The God of Isaac, and The God of Jacob. This profound spiritual connection has been a guiding light in her family's journey, shaping their lives and achievements.

Through her literary works and her thriving bookstore, Pamela continues to inspire readers and promote inclusivity in storytelling, leaving an indelible mark on the world of literature.

www.ingramcontent.com/pod-product-compliance
Lightning Source LLC
Chambersburg PA
CBHW042147200426
43209CB00065B/1778